D0942436

The Case for a
100 Percent Gold Dollar

Murray N. Rothbard

MISES
INSTITUTE

This essay originally appeared in the volume *In Search of a Monetary Constitution*, edited by Leland B. Yeager (Cambridge, Mass.: Harvard University Press, 1962).

Copyright © 2001 by the Ludwig von Mises Institute.

All rights reserved. Written permission must be secured from the publisher to use or reproduce any part of this book, except for brief quotations in critical reviews or articles.

Published by the Ludwig von Mises Institute, 518 West Magnolia Avenue, Auburn, Alabama 36832-4528; www.mises.org.

ISBN: 0-945466-34-X

CONTENTS

Preface

When this essay was published, nearly thirty years ago, America was in the midst of the Bretton Woods system, a Keynesian international monetary system that had been foisted upon the world by the United States and British governments in 1945. The Bretton Woods system was an international dollar standard masquerading as a "gold standard," in order to lend the well-deserved prestige of the world's oldest and most stable money, gold, to the increasingly inflated and depreciated dollar. But this post-World War II system was only a grotesque parody of a gold standard. In the pre-World War I "classical" gold standard, every currency unit, be it dollar, pound, franc, or mark, was defined as a certain unit of weight of gold. Thus, the "dollar" was defined as approximately 1/20 of an ounce of gold, while the pound sterling was defined as a little less than 1/4 of a gold ounce, thus fixing the exchange rate between the two (and between all other currencies) at the ratio of their weights.[1]

Since every national currency was defined as being a certain weight of gold, paper francs or dollars, or

---

[1]The precise ratio of gold weights amounted to defining the pound sterling as equal to $4.86656.

bank deposits were redeemable by the issuer, whether government or bank, in that weight of gold. In particular, these government or bank moneys were redeemable on demand in gold coin, so that the general public could use gold in everyday transactions, providing a severe check upon any temptation to over-issue. The pyramiding of paper or bank credit upon gold was therefore subject to severe limits: the ability by currency holders to redeem those liabilities in gold on demand, whether by citizens of that country or by foreigners. If, in that system, France, for example, inflated the supply of French francs (either in paper or in bank credit), pyramiding more francs on top of gold, the increased money supply and incomes in francs would drive up prices of French goods, making them less competitive in terms of foreign goods, increasing French imports and pushing down French exports, with gold flowing out of France to pay for these balance of payments deficits. But the outflow of gold abroad would put increasing pressure upon the already top-heavy French banking system, even more top-heavy now that the dwindling gold base of the inverted money pyramid was forced to support and back up a greater amount of paper francs. Inevitably, facing bankruptcy, the French banking system would have to contract suddenly, driving down French prices and reversing the gold outflow.

In this way, while the classical gold standard did not prevent boom-bust cycles caused by inflation of money and bank credit, it at least kept that inflation and those cycles in close check.

The Bretton Woods system, an elaboration of the British-induced "gold exchange standard" of the 1920s, was very different. The dollar was defined at 1/35 of a gold ounce; the dollar, however, was only redeemable in large bars of gold bullion by foreign governments and central banks. Nowhere was there redeemability in gold coin; indeed, no private individual or firm could redeem in either coin or bullion. In fact, American citizens were prohibited from owning or holding gold at all, at home or abroad, beyond very small amounts permitted to coin collectors, dentists, and for industrial purposes. None of the other countries' currencies after World War II were either defined or redeemable in gold; instead, they were defined in terms of the dollar, dollars constituting the monetary reserves behind francs, pounds, and marks, and these national money supplies were in turn pyramided on top of dollars.

The result of this system was a seeming bonanza, during the 1940s and 1950s, for American policymakers. The United States was able to issue more paper and credit dollars, while experiencing only small price increases. For as the supply of dollars increased, and the United States experienced the usual balance of payments deficits of inflating countries, other countries, piling up dollar balances, would not, as before 1914, cash them in for gold. Instead, they would accumulate dollar balances and pyramid more francs, lira, etc. on top of them. Instead of each country, then, inflating its own money on top of gold and being severely limited by other countries demanding that gold, these other countries themselves inflated further on top of their increased supply of dollars. The United States was thereby able to "export inflation" to other countries, limiting its own price increases by imposing them on foreigners.

The Bretton Woods system was hailed by Establishment "macroeconomists" and financial experts as sound, noble, and destined to be eternal. The handful of genuine gold standard advocates were derided as "gold bugs," cranks, and Neanderthals. Even the small gold group was split into two parts: the majority, the Spahr group, discussed in this essay, insisted that the Bretton Woods system was right in one crucial respect: that gold was indeed worth $35 an ounce, and that therefore the United States should return to gold at that rate. Misled by the importance of sticking to fixed definitions, the Spahr group insisted on ignoring the fact that the monetary world had changed drastically since 1933, and that therefore the 1933 definition of the dollar being 1/35 of a gold ounce no longer applied to a nation that had not been on a genuine gold standard since that year.[2]

---

[2]Actually, if they had been consistent in their devotion to a fixed definition, the Spahr group should have advocated a return to gold at $20 an ounce, the long-standing definition before Franklin D. Roosevelt began tampering with the gold price in 1933. The "Spahr group" consisted of two organizations: the Economists' National Committee on Monetary Policy, headed by Professor Walter E. Spahr of New York University; and an allied laymen's activist group, headed by Philip McKenna, called The Gold Standard League. Spahr expelled Henry Hazlitt from the former organization for the heresy of advocating return to gold at a far higher price (or lower weight).

The minority of gold standard advocates during the 1960s were almost all friends and followers of the great Austrian school economist Ludwig von Mises. Mises himself, and such men as Henry Hazlitt, DeGaulle's major economic adviser Jacques Rueff, and Michael Angelo Heilperin, pointed out that, as the dollar continued to inflate, it had become absurdly undervalued at $35 an ounce. Gold was worth a great deal more in terms of dollars and other currencies, and the United States, declared the Misesians, should return to a genuine gold standard at a realistic, much higher rate. These Austrian economists were ridiculed by all other schools of economists and financial writers for even mentioning that gold might even be worth the absurdly high price of $70 an ounce. The Misesians predicted that the Bretton Woods system would collapse, since relatively hard money countries, recognizing the continuing depreciation of the dollar, would begin to break the informal gentleman's rules of Bretton Woods and insistently demand redemption in gold that the United States did not possess.

The only other critics of Bretton Woods were the growing wing of Establishment economists, the Friedmanite monetarists. While the monetarists also saw the monetary crises that would be entailed by fixed rates in a world of varying degrees of currency inflation, they were even more scornful of gold than their rivals, the Keynesians. Both groups were committed to a fiat paper standard, but whereas the Keynesians wanted a dollar standard cloaked in a fig-leaf of gold, the monetarists wanted to discard such camouflage, abandon any international money, and simply have national fiat paper moneys freely fluctuating in relation to each other. In short, the Friedmanites were bent on abandoning all the virtues of a world money and reverting to international barter.

Keynesians and Friedmanites alike maintained that the gold bugs were dinosaurs. Whereas Mises and his followers held that gold was giving backing to paper money, both the Keynesian and Friedmanite wings of the Establishment maintained precisely the opposite: that it was sound and solid dollars that were giving value to gold. Gold, both groups asserted, was now worthless as a monetary metal. Cut dollars loose from their artificial connection to gold, they chorused in unison, and we will see that gold will fall to its non-monetary value, then estimated at approximately $6 an ounce.

There can be no genuine laboratory experiments in human affairs, but we came as close as we ever will in 1968, and still more definitively in 1971. Here were two firm and opposing sets of predictions: the Misesians, who stated that if the dollar and gold were cut loose, the price of gold in ever-more inflated dollars would zoom upward; and the massed economic Establishment, from Friedman to Samuelson, and even including such ex-Misesians as Fritz Machlup, maintaining that the price of gold would, if cut free, plummet from $35 to $6 an ounce.

The allegedly eternal system of Bretton Woods collapsed in 1968. The gold price kept creeping above $35 an ounce in the free gold markets of London and Zurich; while the Treasury, committed to maintaining the price of gold at $35, increasingly found itself drained of gold to keep the gold price down. Individual Europeans and other foreigners realized that because of this Treasury commitment, the dollar was, for them, in essence redeemable in gold bullion at $35 an ounce. Since they saw that dollars were really worth a lot less and gold a lot more than that, these foreigners kept accelerating that redemption. Finally, in 1968, the United States and other countries agreed to scuttle much of Bretton Woods, and to establish a "two-tier" gold system. The governments and their central banks would keep the $35 redeemability among themselves as before, but they would seal themselves off hermetically from the pesky free gold market, allowing that price to rise or fall as it may. In 1971, however, the rest of the Bretton Woods system collapsed. Increasingly such hard-money countries as West Germany, France, and Switzerland, getting ever more worried about the depreciating dollar, began to break the gentlemen's rules and insist on redeeming their dollars in gold, as they had a right to do. But as soon as a substantial number of European countries were no longer content to inflate on top of depreciating dollars, and demanded gold instead, the entire system inevitably collapsed. In effect declaring national bankruptcy on August 15, 1971, President Nixon took the United States off the last shred of a gold standard and put an end to Bretton Woods.

Gold and the dollar was thus cut loose in two stages. From 1968 to 1971, governments and their central banks maintained the $35 rate among themselves, while allowing a freely-fluctuating private gold market. From 1971 on, even the fiction of $35 was abandoned.

What then of the laboratory experiment? Flouting all the predictions of the economic Establishment, there was no contest as between themselves and the Misesians: not once did the price of gold on the free market fall below $35. Indeed it kept rising steadily, and after 1971 it vaulted upward, far beyond the once seemingly absurdly high price of $70 an ounce.[3] Here was a clear-cut case where the Misesian forecasts were proven gloriously and spectacularly correct, while the Keynesian and Friedmanite predictions proved to be spectacularly wrong. What, it might well be asked, was the reaction of the Establishment, all allegedly devoted to the view that "science is prediction," and of Milton Friedman, who likes to denounce Austrians for supposedly failing empirical tests? Did he, or they, graciously acknowledge their error and hail Mises and his followers for being right? To ask that question is to answer it. To paraphrase Mencken, that sort of thing will happen the Saturday before the Tuesday before the Resurrection Morn.

---

[3]At one point, the price of gold reached $850, and is now lingering in the area of $350 an ounce. While gold bugs like to mope about the alleged failure of gold to rise still further, it should be noted that even this "depressed" gold price is tenfold the alleged eternally fixed rate of $35 an ounce. One side effect of the rising market price of gold was to ensure the total disappearance of the Spahr group. Thirty-five dollar gold is now not even a legal fiction; it is dead and buried, and it is safe to say that no one, of any school of thought, will want to resurrect it.

After a dramatically unsuccessful and short-lived experiment in fixed exchange rates without any international money, the world has subsisted in a monetarist paradise of national fiat currencies since the spring of 1973. The combination of almost two decades of exchange rate volatility, unprecedentedly high rates of peacetime inflation, and the loss of an international money, have disillusioned the economic Establishment, and induced nostalgia for the once-acknowledged failure of Bretton Woods. One would think that the world would tire of careening back and forth between the various disadvantages of fixed exchange rates with paper money, and fluctuating rates with paper money, and return to a classical, or still better, a 100 percent, gold standard. So far, however, there is no sign of a clamor for gold. The only hope for gold on the monetary horizon, short of a runaway inflation in the United States is the search for a convertible currency in the ruined Soviet Union. It may well dawn on the Russians that their now nearly worthless ruble could be rescued by returning to a genuine gold standard, solidly backed by the large Russian stock of the monetary metal. If so, Russia, in the monetary field, might well end up, ironically, pointing to the West the way to a genuine free-market monetary system.

Two unquestioned articles of faith had been accepted by the entire economic Establishment in 1962. One was a permanent commitment to paper, and scorn for any talk of a gold standard. The other was the uncritical conviction that the American banking system, saved and bolstered by the structure of deposit insurance imposed by the federal government during the New Deal, was as firm as the rock of Gibraltar. Any hint that the American fractional-reserve banking system might be unsound or even in danger, was considered even more crackpot, and more Neanderthal, than a call for return to the gold standard. Once again, both the Keynesian and the Friedmanite wings of the Establishment were equally enthusiastic in endorsing federal deposit insurance and the FDIC (Federal Deposit Insurance Corporation), despite the supposedly fervent Friedmanite adherence to a market economy, free of controls, subsidies, or guarantees. Those of us who raised the alarm against the dangers of fractional-reserve banking were merely crying in the wilderness.

Here again, the landscape has changed drastically in the intervening decades. At first, in the mid-1980s, the fractional-reserve savings and loan banks "insured" by private deposit insurance firms, in Ohio and Maryland, collapsed from massive bank runs. But then, at the end of the 1980s, the entire S&L system went under, necessitating a bailout amounting to hundreds of billions of dollars. The problem was not simply a few banks that had engaged in unsound loans, but runs upon a large part of the S&L system. The result was admitted bankruptcy, and liquidation of the federally operated FSLIC (Federal Savings and Loan Insurance Corporation). FSLIC was precisely to savings and loan banks what the FDIC is to the commercial banking system, and if FSLIC "deposit insurance" can prove to be a hopeless chimera, so too can the long-vaunted FDIC. Indeed, the financial press is filled with stories that the FDIC might well become bankrupt without a further infusion of taxpayer funds. Whereas the "safe" level of FDIC reserves to the deposits it "insures" is alleged to be 1.5 percent, the ratio is now sinking to approximately 0.2 percent, and this is held to be cause for concern.

The important point here is a basic change that has occurred in the psychology of the market and of the public. In contrast to the naive and unquestioning faith of yesteryear, everyone now realizes at least the possibility of collapse of the FDIC. At some point in the possibly near future, perhaps in the next recession and the next spate of bad bank loans, it might dawn upon the public that 1.5 percent is not very safe either, and that no such level can guard against the irresistible holocaust of the bank run. At that point, ignoring the usual mendacious assurances and soothing-syrup of the Establishment, the commercial banks might be plunged into their ultimate crisis. The United States authorities would then be faced with two stark choices. One would be to allow the entire banking system to collapse, along with virtually all the deposits and depositors in that system. Since, given the mind-set of American politicians, and their evident philosophy of "too big to fail," it is certain that they would be forced to embrace the second alternative: massive, hyper-inflationary printing of enough cash to pay off all the bank liabilities. The redeposit of such cash in the banking system would bring about an immediate runaway inflation and a massive flight from the dollar.

Such a future scenario, once seemingly unthinkable, is now definitely on the horizon. Perhaps realization of this plight will lead to increased interest, not only in gold, but also in a 100 percent banking system grounded upon a revalued gold stock.

In one sense, 100 percent banking is now easier to establish than it was in 1962. In my original essay, I called upon the banks to start issuing debentures of varying maturities, which could be purchased by the public and serve as productive channels for genuine savings which would neither be fraudulent nor inflationary. Instead of depositors each believing that they have a total, say, of $1 billion of deposits, while they are all laying claim to only $100 million of reserves, money would be saved and loaned to a bank for a definite term, the bank then relending these savings at an interest differential, and repaying the loan when it becomes due. This is what most people wrongly believe the commercial banks are doing now.

Since the 1960s, however, precisely this system has become widespread in the sale of certificates of deposit (CDs). Everyone is now familiar with purchasing CDs, and demand deposits can far more readily be shifted into CDs than they could have three decades ago. Furthermore, the rise of money market mutual funds (MMMF) in the late 1970s has created another readily available and widely used outlet for savings, outside the commercial banking system. These, too, are a means by which savings are being channelled into short-run credit to business, again without creating new money or generating a boom-bust cycle. Institutionally it would now be easier to shift from fractional to 100 percent reserve banking than ever before.

Unfortunately, now that conditions are riper for 100 percent gold than in several decades, there has been a defection in the ranks of many former Misesians. In a curious flight from gold characteristic of all too many economists in the twentieth century, bizarre schemes have proliferated and gained some currency: for everyone to issue his own "standard money"; for a separation of money as a unit of account from media of exchange; for a government-defined commodity index, and on and on.[4] It is particularly odd that economists who profess to be champions of a free-market economy, should go to such twists and turns to avoid facing the plain fact: that gold, that scarce and valuable market-produced metal, has always been, and will continue to be, by far the best money for human society.

Murray N. Rothbard
Las Vegas, Nevada
September, 1991

---

[4]For a critique of some of these schemes, see Murray N. Rothbard, "Aurophobia, Or: Free Banking On What Standard?", *Review of Austrian Economics* 6, no. 1 (1992): forthcoming; and Rothbard, "The Case for a Genuine Gold Dollar," in Llewellyn H. Rockwell, Jr., ed. *The Gold Standard: An Austrian Perspective* (Lexington, Mass.: Lexington Books, 1985), pp. 1–17.

The Case for
a 100 Percent
Gold Dollar

To advocate the complete, uninhibited gold standard runs the risk, in this day and age, of being classified with the dodo bird. When the Roosevelt administration took us off the gold standard in 1933, the bulk of the nation's economists opposed the move and advocated its speedy restoration. Now gold is considered an absurd anachronism, a relic of a tribal fetish. Gold indeed still retains a certain respectability in international trade; as the pre-eminent international money, gold as a medium of foreign trade can command support. But while foreign trade is important, I would rather choose the far more difficult *domestic* battleground, and argue for a genuine gold standard at home as well as abroad. Yet I shall not join the hardy band of current advocates of the gold standard, who call for a virtual restoration of the status quo *ante* 1933. Although that was a far better monetary system than what we have today, it was not, I hope to show, nearly good enough. By 1932 the gold standard had strayed so far from purity, so far from what it could and should have been, that its weakness contributed signally to its final breakdown in 1933.

Money and Freedom

Economics cannot by itself establish an ethical system, although it provides a great deal of data for anyone constructing such a system—and everyone, in a sense, does so in deciding upon policy. Economists therefore have a responsibility, when advocating policy, to apprise the reader or listener of their ethical position. I do not hesitate to say that my own policy goal is the establishment of the free market, of what used to be called *laissez faire*, as broadly and as purely as possible. For this, I have many reasons, both economic and noneconomic, which I obviously cannot develop here. But I think it important to emphasize that one great desideratum in framing a monetary policy is to find one that is truly compatible with the free market in its widest and fullest sense. This is not only an ethical but also an economic tenet; for, at the very least, the economist who sees the free market working splendidly in all other fields should hesitate for a long time before dismissing it in the sphere of money.

I realize that this is not a popular position to take, even in the most conservative economic circles. Thus, in almost its first sentence, the United States Chamber of Commerce's pamphlet series on "The American Competitive Enterprise Economy" announced: "Money is what the government says it is."[1] It is almost universally

---

[1] Economic Research Department, Chamber of Commerce of the United States, *The Mystery of Money* (Washington, D.C.: Chamber of Commerce, 1953), p. 1.

believed that money, at least, cannot be free; that it must be controlled, regulated, manipulated, and created by government. Aside from the more strictly economic criticisms that I will have of this view, we should keep in mind that money, in any market economy advanced beyond the stage of primitive barter, is the nerve center of the economic system. If, therefore, the state is able to gain unquestioned control over the unit of all accounts, the state will then be in a position to dominate the entire economic system, and the whole society. It will also be able to add quietly and effectively to its own wealth and to the wealth of its favorite groups, and without incurring the wrath that taxes often invoke. The state has understood this lesson since the kings of old began repeatedly to debase the coinage.

The Dollar:
Independent Name or
Unit of Weight?

"If you favor a free market, why in the world do you say that government should fix the price of gold?" And, "If you wish to tie the dollar to a commodity, why not a market basket of commodities instead of only gold?" These questions are often asked of the libertarian who favors a gold standard; but the very framing of the questions betrays a fundamental misconception of the nature of money and of the gold standard. For the crucial, implicit assumption of such questions—and of nearly all current thinking on the subject of money—is that "dollars" are an independent entity. If dollars are indeed properly things-in-themselves, to be bought, sold, and evaluated on the market, then it is surely true that "fixing the price of gold" in terms of dollars becomes simply an act of government intervention.

There is, of course, no question about the fact that, in the world of today, dollars are an independent entity, as are pounds of sterling, francs, marks, and escudos. If this were all, and if we simply accepted the fact of such independence and did not inquire beyond, then I would be happy to join Professors Milton Friedman, Leland Yeager, and others of the Chicago school, and call for cutting these independent national moneys loose from arbitrary exchange rates fixed by government and allowing a freely fluctuating market in foreign exchange. But the point is that I do not think that these national moneys should be independent entities. Why they should not stems from the very nature and essence of money and of the market economy.

The market economy and the modern world's system of division of labor operate as follows: a producer supplies a good or a service, selling it for money; he then uses the money to buy other goods or services that he needs. Let us then consider a hypothetical world of pure *laissez faire*, where the market functions freely and government has not infringed at all upon the monetary sphere. This system of selling goods for money would then be the only way by which an individual could acquire the money that he needed to obtain goods and services. The process would be:

production $\longrightarrow$ "purchase" of money $\longrightarrow$ "sale" of money for goods.[2]

To those advocates of independent paper moneys who also champion the free market, I would address this simple question: "Why don't you advocate the unlimited freedom of each individual to manufacture dollars?" If dollars are really and properly things-in-themselves, why not let everyone manufacture them as they manufacture wheat and baby food? It is obvious that there is indeed something peculiar about such money. For if everyone had the right to print paper dollars, everyone would print them in unlimited amounts, the costs being minuscule compared to the almost infinitely large denominations that could be printed upon the notes. Clearly, the entire monetary system would break down completely. If paper dollars are to be the "standard" money, then almost everyone would admit that government must step in and acquire compulsory monopoly of money creation so as to check its unlimited increase. There is something else wrong with everyone printing his own dollars: for then the chain from production of goods through "purchase" of money to "sale" of money for goods would be broken, and anyone could create money without having to be a producer first. He could consume without

---

[2]A person could also receive money from producers by inheritance or other gift, but here again the ultimate giver must have been a producer. Furthermore, we may say that the recipient "produced" some intangible service—for instance, of being a son and heir— which provided the reason for the giver's contribution.

producing, and thus seize the output of the economy from the genuine producers.

Government's compulsory monopoly of dollar-creation does not solve all these problems, however, and even makes new ones. For what is there to prevent *government* from creating money at its own desired pace, and thereby benefiting itself and its favored citizens? Once again, nonproducers can create money without producing and obtain resources at the expense of the producers. Furthermore, the historical record of governments can give no one confidence that they will not do precisely that —even to the extent of hyperinflation and chaotic breakdown of the currency.

Why is it that, historically, the relatively free market never had to worry about people wildly setting up money factories and printing unlimited quantities?[3] If "money" really means dollars and pounds and francs, then this would surely have been a problem. But the nub of the issue is this: On the pristine free market, money does not and cannot mean the names of paper tickets. Money means a certain commodity, previously useful for other purposes on the market, chosen over the years by that market as an especially useful and marketable commodity to serve as a medium for exchanges. No one prints dollars on the purely free market because *there are, in fact, no dollars*; there are only commodities, such as wheat, automobiles, and gold. In barter, commodities

---

[3]The American "wildcat bank" did not print money itself, but rather bank notes supposedly *redeemable* in money.

are exchanged for each other, and then, gradually, a particularly marketable commodity is increasingly used as a medium of exchange. Finally, it achieves general use as a medium and becomes a "money." I need not go through the familiar but fascinating story of how gold and silver were selected by the market after it had discarded such commodity moneys as cows, fishhooks, and iron hoes.[4] And I need also not dwell on the unique qualities possessed by gold and silver that caused the market to select them—those qualities lovingly enunciated by all the older textbooks on money: high marketability, durability, portability, recognizability, and homogeneity. Like every other commodity, the "price" of gold in terms of the commodities it can buy varies in accordance with its supply and demand. Since the demand for gold and silver was high, and since their supply was low in relation to the demand, the value of each unit in terms of other goods was high—a most useful attribute of money. This scarcity, combined with great durability, meant that the annual fluctuations of supply were necessarily small—another useful feature of a money commodity.

Commodities on the market exchange by their unit weights, and gold and silver were no exceptions. When someone sold copper to buy gold and then to buy butter, he sold *pounds* of copper for *ounces* or *grams* of gold to

---

[4]On the process of emergence of money on the market, see the classic exposition of Carl Menger in his *Principles of Economics*, translated and edited by James Dingwall and Bert F. Hoselitz (Glencoe, Ill.: Free Press, 1950), pp. 257–85.

buy pounds of butter. On the free market, therefore, the monetary unit—the unit of the nation's accounts—naturally emerges as the unit of weight of the money commodity, for example, the silver ounce, or the gold gram.

In this monetary system emerging on the free market, no one can create money out of thin air to acquire resources from the producers. Money can only be obtained by purchasing it with one's goods or services. The only exception to this rule is gold miners, who can produce new money. But they must invest resources in finding, mining, and transporting an especially scarce commodity. Furthermore, gold miners are productively adding to the world's stock of gold for nonmonetary uses as well.

Let us indeed assume that gold has been selected as the general medium of exchange by the market, and that the unit of account is the gold gram. What will be the consequences of complete monetary freedom for each individual? What of the freedom of the individual to print his own money, which we have seen to be so disastrous in our age of fiat paper? First, let us remember that the gold gram is the monetary unit, and that such debasing names as "dollar," "franc," and "mark" do not exist and have never existed. Suppose that I decided to abandon the slow, difficult process of producing services for money, or of mining money, and instead decided to print my own? What would I print? I might manufacture a paper ticket, and print upon it "10 Rothbards." I could then proclaim the ticket as "money," and enter a store to purchase groceries with my embossed Rothbards. In the purely free market which I advocate, I or anyone else would have a perfect right to do this. And what would be the inevitable consequence? Obviously, that no one would pay attention to the Rothbards, which would be properly treated as an arrogant joke. The same would be true of any "Joneses," "Browns," or paper tickets printed by anyone else. And it should be clear that the problem is not simply that few people have ever heard of me. If General Motors tried to pay its workers in paper tickets entitled "50 GMs," the tickets would gain as little response. None of these tickets would be money, and none would be considered as anything but valueless, except perhaps a few collectors of curios. And this is why total freedom for everyone to print money would be absolutely harmless in a purely free market: no one would accept these presumptuous tickets.

Why not freely fluctuating exchange rates? Fine, let us have freely fluctuating exchange rates on our completely free market; let the Rothbards and Browns and GM's fluctuate at whatever rate they will exchange for gold or for each other. The trouble is that they would never reach this exalted state because they would never gain acceptance in exchange as moneys at all, and therefore the problem of exchange rates would never arise.

On a really free market, then, there would be freely fluctuating exchange rates, but only between genuine commodity moneys, since the paper-name moneys could never gain enough acceptance to enter the field. Specifically, since gold and silver have historically been the leading commodity moneys, gold and silver would probably both be moneys, and would exchange at freely fluctuating rates. Different groups and communities of people would pick one or the other money as their unit of accounting.[5]

[5]The exchange rate between gold and silver will inevitably be at or near their purchasing-power parities, in terms of the social array of goods available, and this rate would tend to be uniform throughout the world. For a brilliant exposition of the nature of the geographic purchasing power of money, and the theory of purchasing-power parity, see Ludwig von Mises, *The Theory of Money and Credit*, 2d ed. (New Haven: Yale University Press, 1953), pp. 170–86. Also see Chi-Yuen Wu, *An Outline of International Price Theories* (London: Routledge, 1939), pp. 233–34.

Since I am advocating a totally free market in money, what I am strictly proposing is not so much the gold standard as parallel gold and silver standards. By this, of course, I do not mean bimetallism, with its arbitrarily fixed exchange rate between gold and silver, but freely fluctuating exchange rates between the two moneys. For an illuminating account of how parallel standards worked historically and how they were interfered with, see Luigi Einaudi, "The Theory of Imaginary Money from Charlemagne to the French Revolution," in Frederic C. Lane and Jelle C. Riemersma, eds., *Enterprise and Secular Change* (Homewood, Ill.: Irwin, 1953), pp. 229–61.

Professor Robert Sabatino Lopez writes, of the return of Europe to gold coinage in the mid-thirteenth century, after half a millennium: "Florence, like most medieval states, made bimetallism and trimetallism a base of its monetary policy . . . it committed the government to the Sysiphean labor of readjusting the relations between different coins as the ratio between the different metals changes, or as one or another coin was debased . . . Genoa, on the contrary, *in conformity with the principle of restricting state intervention as much as possible* [italics mine], did not try to enforce a fixed relation between coins of different metals . . . Basically, the gold coinage of Genoa was not meant to integrate the silver and billon coinages but to form an independent system" ("Back to Gold, 1251," *Economic History Review* [April 1956]: 224).

On the merits of parallel standards and their superiority to bimetallism, see William Brough, *Open Mints and Free Banking* (New York: Putnam, 1898), and Brough, *The Natural Law of Money* (New

Names, therefore, whatever they may be, "Rothbard," "Jones," or even "dollar," could not have arisen as money on the free market. How, then did such names as "dollar" and "peso" originate and emerge in their own right as independent moneys? The answer is that *these names invariably originated as names for units of weight of a money commodity, either gold or silver.* In short, they began not as pure names, but as names of units of weight of particular money commodities. In the British pound sterling we have a particularly striking example of a weight derivative, for the British pound was originally just that: a pound of silver money.[6] "Dollar" began as the generally applied name of an ounce weight of silver coined in the sixteenth century by a Bohemian, Count Schlick, who lived in Joachimsthal, and the name of his highly reputed coins became "Joachimsthalers," or simply "thalers" or "dollars." And even after a lengthy process of debasement, alteration, and manipulation of

---

York: Putnam, 1894). Brough called this system "Free Metallism." On the recent example of pure parallel standards in Saudi Arabia, down to the 1950s, see Arthur N. Young, "Saudi Arabian Currency and Finance," *Middle East Journal* (Summer 1953): 361–80.

[6]The fact that there was never an actual pound-weight coin of silver is irrelevant and does not imply that the pound was some form of "imaginary" unit of account. The pound was a pound of silver bullion, or an accumulation of a pound weight of silver coins. Cf. Einaudi, "Theory of Imaginary Money," pp. 229–30. The fundamental misconception here is to place too much emphasis on coins and not enough on bullion, an overemphasis, as we shall see presently, connected intimately with government intervention and with the long slide downward of the monetary unit from weight of gold and silver to pure name.

these weights until they more and more became separated names, they still remained names of units of weight of specie until, in the United States, we went off the gold standard in 1933. In short, it is incorrect to say that, before 1933, the price of gold was fixed in terms of dollars. Instead, what happened was that the dollar was *defined* as a unit of weight, approximately 1/20 of an ounce of gold. It is not that the dollar was set equal to a certain weight of gold; it *was* that weight, just as any unit of weight, as, for example, one pound of copper *is* 16 ounces of copper, and is not simply and arbitrarily "set equal" to 16 ounces by some individual or agency.[7] The monetary unit was, therefore, always a unit of weight of a money commodity, and the names that we know now as independent moneys were names of these units of weight.[8]

---

[7]The monetary unit was not just a pure unit of weight, such as the ounce or the gram; it was a unit of weight of a certain money commodity, such as gold. The dollar was 1/20 of an ounce of *gold*, not of just any ounce. And here we find a crucial flaw in the idea of a composite-commodity money which has been overlooked: Just as we cannot call the monetary unit an "ounce" or "gram" or "pound" of several different, or composite, commodities, so the dollar cannot properly be the *name* of many different weights of many different commodities. The money commodity selected by the market was a single particular commodity, gold or silver, and therefore the *unit* of that money had to be of that commodity alone, and not of some arbitrary composite.

[8]This is why, in the older books, a discussion of money and monetary standards often take place as part of a general discussion of weights and measures. Thus in Barnard's work on international unification of weights and measures, the problem of international unification of monetary units was discussed in an appendix, along with other appendixes on measures of capacity and metric system. Frederick A. P. Barnard, *The Metric System of Weights and Measures*, rev. ed. (New York: Columbia College, 1872).

Murray N. Rothbard

Economists, of course, admit that our modern national moneys emerged originally from gold and silver, but they are inclined to dismiss this process as a historical accident from which we have now been happily emancipated. But Ludwig von Mises has shown, in his regression theorem, that logically money can only originate in a nonmonetary commodity, chosen gradually by the market to be an ever more general medium of exchange. Money cannot originate as a new fiat name, either by government edict or by some form of social compact. The basic reason is that the demand for money on any "day," X, which along with the supply of money determines the purchasing power of the money unit on that "day," itself depends on the very existence of a purchasing power on the previous "day," X-1. For while every other commodity on the market is useful in its own right, money (or a monetary commodity considered in its strictly *monetary* use), is only useful to *exchange* for other goods and services. Hence, alone among goods, money depends for its use and demand on having a pre-existing purchasing power. Since this is true for any "day" when money exists, we can push the logical regression backward, to see that ultimately the money commodity must have had a use in the "days" previous to money, that is, in the world of barter.[9]

[9]Ludwig von Mises developed the very important regression theorem in his *Theory of Money and Credit*, pp. 97–123, and defended it against the criticisms of Benjamin M. Anderson and Howard S. Ellis in his *Human Action* (New Haven: Yale University Press, 1949), pp. 405–08. Also see Joseph A. Schumpeter, *History of Economic*

I want to make it clear what I am *not* saying. I am not saying that fiat money, once established on the ruins of gold, cannot then continue indefinitely on its own. Unfortunately, such ultrametallists as J. Laurence Laughlin were wrong; indeed, if fiat money could not continue indefinitely, I would not have to come here to plead for its abolition.

The Decline from Weight to Name: Monopolizing the Mint

The debacle of 1931–1933, when the world abandoned the gold standard, was not a sudden shift from gold weight to paper name; it was but the last step in a lengthy, complex process. It is important, not just for historical reasons but for framing public policy today, to

---

Analysis (New York: Oxford University Press, 1954), p. 1090. For a reply to Professor J. C. Gilbert's contention that the establishment of the *Rentenmark* disproved the regression theorem, see Murray N. Rothbard, "Toward a Reconstruction of Utility and Welfare Economics," in Mary Sennholz, ed., *On Freedom and Free Enterprise* (Princeton: Van Nostrand, 1956), p. 236n.

The latest criticism of the regression theorem is that of Professor Patinkin, who accuses Mises of inconsistency in basing this theorem on deriving the marginal utility of money from the marginal utility of the goods that it will purchase, rather than from the marginal utility of cash holdings, the latter approach being used by Mises in the remainder of his work. Actually, the regression theorem in Mises's system is not inconsistent, but operates on a different plane, for it shows that the very marginal utility of money *to hold*—as elsewhere analyzed by Mises—is itself based upon the *prior* fact that money has a purchasing power *in goods*. Don Patinkin, *Money, Interest, and Prices* (Evanston, Ill.: Row, Peterson, 1956), pp. 71–72, 414.

analyze the logical steps in this transformation. Each stage of this process was caused by another act of government intervention.

On the market, commodities take different forms for different uses, and so, on a free market, would gold or silver. The basic form of processed gold is gold bullion, and ingots or bars of bullion would be used for very large transactions. For smaller, everyday transactions, the gold would be divided into smaller pieces, coins, hardened by the slight infusion into an alloy to prevent abrasion (accounted for in the final weight). It should be understood that all forms of gold would really be money, since gold exchanges by weight. A gold ornament is itself money as well as ornament; it could be used in exchange, but it is simply not in a convenient shape for exchanges, and would probably be melted back into bullion before being used as money. Even sacks of gold dust might be used for exchange in mining towns. Of course it costs resources to shift gold from one form to another, and therefore on the market coins would tend to be at a premium over the equivalent weight in bullion, since it generally costs more to produce a coin out of bullion than to melt coins back into bullion.

The first and most crucial act of government intervention in the market's money was its assumption of the compulsory monopoly of minting—the process of transforming bullion into coin. The pretext for socialization of minting—one which has curiously been accepted by almost every economist—is that private minters would defraud the public on the weight and fineness of the coins. This argument rings peculiarly hollow when we consider the long record of governmental debasement of the coinage and of the monetary standard. But apart from this, we certainly know that private enterprise has been able to supply an almost infinite number of goods requiring high precision standards; yet nobody advocates nationalization of the machine-tool industry or the electronics industry in order to safeguard these standards. And no one wants to abolish all contracts because some people might commit fraud in making them. Surely the proper remedy for any fraud is the general law in defense of property rights.[10]

---

[10]Presumably, on the free market private citizens will also safeguard their coins by testing their weight and purity—as they do their monetary bullion—or will mint coins with those private minters who have established reputations for probity and efficiency.

Even in the heyday of the gold standard there were few writers willing to go beyond the bounds of social habit to concede the feasibility of private minting. A notable exception was Herbert Spencer, *Social Statics* (New York: Appleton, 1890), pp. 438–39. The French economist Paul Leroy-Beaulieu also favored free private coinage. See Charles A. Conant, *The Principles of Money and Banking* (New York: Harper, 1905), vol. 1, pp. 127–28. Also see Leonard E. Read, *Government—An Ideal Concept* (Irvington-on-Hudson, N.Y.: Foundation for Economic Education, 1954), pp. 82ff. Recently Professor Milton Friedman, though completely out of sympathy with the gold standard, has, remarkably, taken a similar stand in *A Program for Monetary Stability* (New York: Fordham University Press, 1960), p. 5.

For historical examples of successful private coinage, see B. W. Barnard, "The Use of Private Tokens for Money in the United States," *Quarterly Journal of Economics* (1916–17): 617–26; Conant, vol. 1, pp. 127–32; Lysander Spooner, *A Letter to Grover Cleveland* (Boston: Tucker, 1886), p. 69; and J. Laurence Laughlin, *A New Exposition of Money, Credit and Prices* (Chicago: University of Chicago Press, 1931), vol. 1, pp. 47–51.

The standard argument against private coinage is that the minting business operates by a mysterious law of its own—Gresham's Law—where "bad money drives out good," in contrast to other areas of competition, where the good product drives out the bad.[11] But Mises has brilliantly shown that this formulation of Gresham's Law is a misinterpretation, and that the Law is a subdivision of the usual effects of price control by government: in this case, the government's artificial fixing of an exchange rate between two or more moneys creates a shortage of the artificially under-valued money and a surplus of the over-valued money. Gresham's Law is therefore a law of government intervention rather than one of the free market.[12]

The state's nationalization of the minting business injured the free market and the monetary system in many ways. One neglected point is that government minting is subject to the same flaws, inefficiencies, and tyranny over the consumer as every other government operation. Since coins are a convenient monetary shape for daily transactions, the state's decree that only X, Y,

[11]Thus, see W. Stanley Jevons's criticism of Spencer in his *Money and the Mechanism of Exchange*, 15th ed. (London: Kegan Paul, 1905), pp. 63–66.

[12]See Mises, *Human Action*, pp. 432n, 447, 754. Mises was partly anticipated at the turn of the century by William Brough: "The more efficient money will always drive from the circulation the less efficient if the individuals who handle money are left free to act in their own interest. It is only when bad money is endorsed by the State with the property of legal tender that it can drive good money from circulation" (*Open Mints and Free Banking*, pp. 35–36).

and Z denominations shall be coined imposes a loss of utility on consumers and substitutes uniformity for the diversity of the market. It also begins the long disastrous slide from an emphasis on weight to an emphasis on name, or tale. In short, under private coinage there would be a number of denominations, in strict accordance with the variety of consumer wants. The private stamp would probably guarantee fineness rather than weight, and the coins would circulate by weight. But if the government decrees just a few denominations, then weight begins to be disregarded, and the name of the coin to be considered more and more. For example, the problem persisted in Europe for centuries of what to do with old, worn coins. If a 30-gram coin was worn down to 25 grams, the simplest thing would be for the old coin to circulate *not* at the old and now misleading 30 grams but at the new, correct 25 grams. The fact that the state itself had stamped 30 grams on the new coin, however, was somehow considered an insuperable barrier to such a simple solution. And, futhermore, much monetary debasement took place through the state's decree that new and old coins be treated alike, with Gresham's Law causing new coins to be hoarded and only old ones to circulate.[13]

---

[13]The minting monopoly also permitted the state to charge a monopoly price ("seigniorage") for its minting service, which imposed a special burden on conversion from bullion to coin. In later years the state granted the subsidy of costless coinage, overstimulating the transformation of bullion to coin. Modern adherents of the gold standard unfortunately endorse the subsidy of gratuitous coinage. Where coinage is private and marketable, the firms will of course charge a fee covering approximately the true costs of minting (such a fee is known as "brassage").

The royal stamp on coins also gradually shifted emphasis from weight to tale by wrapping coinage in the trappings of the mystique of state "sovereignty." For many centuries it was considered no disgrace for foreign gold and silver coins to circulate in any area; monetary nationalism was yet in its infancy. The United States used foreign coins almost exclusively through the first quarter of the nineteenth century. But gradually foreign coins were outlawed, and the name of the national state's unit became enormously more significant.

Debasement through the centuries greatly spurred a loss of confidence in money as a unit of weight. There is only one point to any standard of weight: that it be eternally fixed. The international meter must always be the international meter. But using their minting monopoly, the state rulers juggled standards of monetary weight to their own economic advantage. It was as if the state were a huge warehouse that had accepted many pounds of copper or other commodity from its clients, and then, when the clients came to redeem, the warehouseman suddenly announced that henceforth a pound would equal 12 ounces instead of 16, and paid out only three fourths of the copper, pocketing the other fourth for his own use. It is perhaps superfluous to point out that any private agency doing such a thing would be promptly branded as criminal.[14]

---

[14]Besides the minting monopoly, the other critical device for government control of money has been legal-tender laws, superfluous at best, mischievous and a means of arbitrary exchange-rate fixing

The Decline from Weight to Name: Encouraging Bank Inflation

The natural tendency of the state is inflation. This statement will shock those accustomed to viewing the state as a committee of the whole nation ardently dispensing the general welfare, but I think it nonetheless true. The reason seems to be obvious. As I have mentioned above, money is acquired on the market by producing goods and services, and then buying money in exchange for these goods. But there is another way to obtain money: creating money oneself, without producing—by counterfeiting. Money creation is a much less costly method than producing; therefore the state, with its ever-tightening monopoly of money creation, has a simple route that it can take to benefit its own members and its favored supporters.[15] And it is a more enticing

---

at worst. As William Brough stated: "There is no more case for a special law to compel the receiving of money than there is for one to compel the receiving of wheat or of cotton. The common law is as adequate for the enforcement of contracts in the one case as in the other" (*The Natural Law of Money*, p. 135). The same position was taken by T. H. Farrer, *Studies in Currency, 1898* (London: Macmillan, 1898), pp. 42ff.

[15]This is a corollary of Franz Oppenheimer's brilliant distinction between the two basic alternate routes to wealth, production and exchange, which he called "the economic means"; and seizure or confiscation, which he called "the political means." Inflation, which I am defining here as the creation of money (i.e., an increase of money substitutes not backed 100 percent by standard specie), is thus revealed as one of the major political means. Oppenheimer defined the state, incidentally, as the "organization of the political means" (*The State* [New York: Vanguard Press, 1926], pp. 24ff).

and less disturbing route than taxes—which might provoke open opposition. Creating money, on the contrary, confers open and evident benefits on those who create and first receive it; the losses it imposes on the rest of society remain hidden to the lay observer. This tendency of the state should alone preclude all the schemes of economists and other writers for government to issue and stabilize the supply of paper money.

While countries were still on a specie standard, bank notes and government paper were issued as redeemable in specie. They were money substitutes, essentially warehouse receipts for gold, that could be redeemed in face value on demand. Soon, however, the issue of receipts went beyond 100 percent reserve to outright money creation. Governments have persistently tried their best to promote, encourage, and expand the circulation of bank and government paper, and to discourage the people's use of gold itself. Any individual bank has two great checks on its creation of money: a call for redemption by non-clients (that is, by clients of other banks, or by those who wish to use standard money), and a crisis of confidence in the bank by its clients, causing a "run." Governments have continually operated to widen these limits, which would be narrow in a system of "free banking"—a system where banks are free to do anything they please, so long as they promptly redeem their obligations to pay specie. They have created a central bank to widen the limits to the whole country by permitting all banks to inflate together—under the tutelage of the government. And they have tried to assure the banks that the government will not permit them to fail, either by coining the convenient doctrine that the central bank must be a "lender of last resort" or reserves to the banks, or, as in America, by simply "suspending specie payments," that is, by permitting banks to continue operations while refusing to redeem their contractual obligations to pay specie.[16]

[16]It is a commonly accepted myth that the excess of wildcat banks in America stemmed from free banking; actually, a much stronger cause was the tradition, beginning in 1814 and continuing in every economic crisis thereafter, of permitting banks to continue in operation without paying in specie.

It is also a widespread myth that central banks are inaugurated in order to *check* inflation by commercial banks. The second Bank of the United States, on the contrary, was inaugurated in 1817 as an inflationist sop to the state-chartered banks, which had been permitted to run riot without paying in specie since 1814. It was a weak substitute for compelling a genuine return to specie payments. This was correctly pointed out at the time by such hard-money stalwarts as Daniel Webster and John Randolph of Roanoke. Senator William H. Wells, Federalist of Delaware, said that the Bank Bill was "ostensibly for the purpose of correcting the diseased state of our paper currency by restraining and curtailing the overissue of bank paper, and yet it came prepared to inflict upon us the same evil; being itself nothing more than simply a paper-making machine." *Annals of Congress*, 14 Cong., 1 Sess., April 1, 1816, pp. 267–70. Also see ibid., pp. 1066, 1091, 1110ff.

As for the Federal Reserve System, the major arguments for its adoption were to make the money supply more "elastic" and to centralize reserves and thus make them more "efficient," i.e., to facilitate and promote inflation. As an additional fillip, reserve requirements themselves were directly lowered at the inauguration of the Federal Reserve System. Cf. the important but totally neglected work of C. A. Phillips, T. F. McManus, and R. W. Nelson, *Banking and the Business Cycle* (New York: Macmillan, 1937), pp. 21ff, and passim. Also see O. K. Burrel, "The Coming Crisis in External Convertibility in U. S. Gold," *Commercial and Financial Chronicle* (April 23, 1959): 5.

For a discussion of the historical arguments on free or central banking see Vera C. Smith, *The Rationale of Central Banking* (London: King, 1936).

Another device used over the years by governments was to persuade the public not to use gold in their daily transactions; to do so was scorned as an anachronism unsuited to the modern world. The yokel who didn't trust banks became a common object of ridicule. In this way, gold was more and more confined to the banks and to use for very large transactions; this made it very much easier to go off the gold standard during the Great Depression, for then the public could be persuaded that the only ones to suffer were a few selfish, antisocial, and subtly unpatriotic gold hoarders. In fact, as early as the Panic of 1819 the idea had spread that someone trying to redeem his bank note in specie, that is, to redeem his own property, was a subversive citizen trying to wreck the banks and the entire economy; and by the 1930s it was thus easy to denounce gold hoarders as virtual traitors.[17]

---

[17]During the Panic the economist Condy Raguet, state senator from Philadelphia, wrote to a puzzled David Ricardo as follows: "You state in your letter that you find it difficult to comprehend, why persons who had a right to demand coin from the Banks in payment of their notes, so long forbore to exercise it. This no doubt appears paradoxical to one who resides in a country where an act of parliament was necessary to protect a bank, but the difficulty is easily solved. The whole of our population are either stockholders of banks or in debt to them.... An independent man, who was neither a stockholder or debtor, who would have ventured to compel the banks to do justice, would have been persecuted as an enemy of society. . . ." Raguet to Ricardo, April 18, 1821, in David Ricardo, *Minor Papers on the Currency Question, 1809–23*, ed. Jacob Hollander (Baltimore, Maryland: The Johns Hopkins Press, 1932), pp. 199–201.

In 1931, for example, President Hoover launched a crusade against "traitorous hoarding." The crusade consisted of the Citizens' Reconstruction Organization, headed by Colonel Frank Knox of

And so by imposing central banking, by suspending specie payments, and by encouraging a shift among the public from gold to paper or bank deposits in their everyday transactions, the governments organized inflation, and thus an ever larger proportion of money substitutes to gold (an increasing proportion of liabilities redeemable on demand in gold, to gold itself). By the 1930s, in short, the gold standard—a shaky gold base supporting an ever greater pyramid of monetary claims—was ready to collapse at the first severe depression or wave of bank runs.[18]

100 Percent Gold Banking

We have thus come to the cardinal difference between myself and the bulk of those economists who still advocate

---

Chicago. And Jesse Jones reports that, during the banking crisis of early 1933, Hoover was seriously contemplating invoking a forgotten wartime law making hoarding a criminal offense. Jesse H. Jones and Edward Angly, *Fifty Billion Dollars* (New York: Macmillan, 1951), p. 18. It should also be noted here that the Hoover administration's alleged devotion to retaining the gold standard is largely myth. As Hoover's Undersecretary of the Treasury has declared rather proudly: "The going off [gold] cannot be laid to Franklin Roosevelt. It had been determined to be necessary by Ogden Mills, Secretary of the Treasury, and myself as his Undersecretary, long before Franklin Roosevelt took office." Arthur A. Ballantine, in the *New York Herald-Tribune*, May 5, 1958, p. 18.

[18]Currently, the worst example of government aid to banks is the highly popular deposit insurance—for this means that banks have virtual carte blanche from government to protect them from any redemption crisis. As a result, virtually all natural market checks on bank inflation have been destroyed. Query: If banks are thus protected from losses by government, to what extent are they still private institutions?

a return to the gold standard. These economists, represented by Dr. Walter E. Spahr and his associates in the Economists' National Committee on Monetary Policy, essentially believe that the old pre-1933 gold standard was a fine and viable institution in all its parts, and that going off gold in 1933 was a single wicked act of will that only needs to be repealed in order to re-establish our monetary system on a sound foundation. I, on the contrary, view 1933 as but the last link in a whole chain of unfortunate actions; it seems clear to me that the gold standard of the 1920s was so vitiated as to be ready to collapse. A return to such a gold standard, while superior to the present system, would only pave the way for another collapse—and this time, I am afraid, gold would get no further chance. Although the transition period would be more difficult, it would be kinder to the gold standard, as well as better for the long-run economic health of the country, to go back to a stronger, more viable gold standard than the one we have lost.

I daresay that my audience has been too much exposed to the teachings of the Chicago School to be shocked at the idea of 100 percent reserve banking. This topic, of course, is worthy of far more space than I can give it here. I can only say that my position on 100 percent banking differs considerably in emphasis from the Chicago School. The Chicago group basically views 100 percent money as a technique—as a useful, efficient tool for government manipulation of the money supply, unburdened by lags or friction in the banking system. My reasons for advocating 100 percent banking cut much closer to the heart of our whole system of the free market and property rights.[19] In my view, issuing promises to pay on demand in excess of the amount of goods on hand is simply fraud, and should be so considered by the legal system. For this means that a bank issues "fake" warehouse receipts—warehouse receipts, for example, for ounces of gold that do not actually exist in the vaults. This is legalized counterfeiting; this is the creation of money without the necessity for production, to compete for resources against those who have produced. In short, I believe that fractional-reserve banking is disastrous both for the morality and for the fundamental bases and institutions of the market economy.

I am familiar with the many arguments for fractional-reserve banking. There is the view that this is simply economical: The banks began with 100 percent reserves, but then they shrewdly and keenly saw that only a certain proportion of these demand liabilities were likely to be redeemed, so that it seemed safe either to lend out the gold for profit or to issue pseudo-warehouse receipts (either as bank notes or as bank deposits) for the gold, and to lend out those. The banks here take on the character of shrewd entrepreneurs. But so is an embezzler shrewd when he takes money out

---

[19]The other very important difference, of course, is that I advocate 100 percent reserves in gold or silver, in contrast to the 100 percent fiat paper standard of the Chicago School. One-hundred percent gold, rather than making the monetary system more readily manageable by government, would completely expunge government intervention from the monetary system.

of the company till to invest in some ventures of his own. Like the banker, he sees an opportunity to earn a profit on *someone else's* assets. The embezzler knows, let us say, that the auditor will come on June 1 to inspect the accounts; and he fully intends to repay the "loan" before then. Let us assume that he does; is it really true that no one has been the loser and everyone has gained? I dispute this; a theft has occurred, and that theft should be prosecuted and not condoned. Let us note that the banking advocate assumes that something has gone wrong only if everyone should decide to redeem his property, only to find that it isn't there. But I maintain that the wrong—the theft—occurs at the time the embezzler takes the money, not at the later time when his "borrowing" happens to be discovered.[20]

Another argument holds that the fact that notes and deposits are redeemable on demand is only a kind of accident; that these are merely credit transactions. The depositors or noteholders are simply lending money to the banks, which in turn act as their agents to channel the money to business firms. And why repress productive credit? Mises has shown, however, the crucial difference between a *credit transaction* and a *claim transaction*; credit always involves the purchase of a

[20]I want to make it quite clear that I do not accuse present-day bankers of conscious fraud or embezzlement; the institution of banking has become so hallowed and venerated that we can only say that it allows for legalized fraud, probably unknown to almost all bankers. As for the original goldsmiths that began the practice, I think our opinion should be rather more harsh.

future good by the creditor in exchange for a present good (money). The creditor gives up a present good in exchange for an IOU for a good coming to him in the future. But a claim—and bank notes or deposits are claims to money—does not involve the creditor's relinquishing any of the present good. On the contrary, the noteholder or deposit-holder still retains his money (the present good) because he has a claim to it, a warehouse receipt, which he can redeem at any time he desires.[21] This is the nub of the problem, and this is why fractional-reserve banking creates new money while other credit agencies do not—for warehouse receipts or claims to money function on the market as equivalent to standard money itself.

To those who persist in believing that the bulk of bank deposits are really saved funds voluntarily left

---

[21]"It is usual to reckon the acceptance of a deposit which can be drawn upon at any time by means of note or checks as a type of credit transaction and juristically, this view is, of course, justified; but economically, the case is not one of a credit transaction. If *credit* in the economic sense means the exchange of a present good or a present service against a future good or a future service, then it is hardly possible to include the transactions in question under the conception of credit. A depositor of a sum of money who acquires in exchange for it a claim convertible into money at any time which will perform exactly the same service for him as the sum it refers to has exchanged no present good for a future good. The claim that he has acquired by his deposit is also a present good for him. The depositing of money in no way means that he has renounced immediate disposal over the utility that it commands." Mises, *The Theory of Money and Credit*, p. 268. What I am advocating, in brief, is a change in the juristic framework to conform to the economic realities.

with the banks to invest for savers, and are not just kept as monetary cash balances, I would like to lay down this challenge: If what you say is true, why not agree to alter the banking structure to change these deposits to debentures of varying maturities? A shift from uncovered deposits to debentures will of course mean an enormous drop in the supply of money; but if these deposits are simply another form of credit, then the depositors should not object and we 100-percent theorists will be satisfied. The purchase of a debenture will, furthermore, be a genuine saving and investment of existing money, rather than an unsound increase in the money supply.[22]

In sum, I am advocating that the law be changed to treat bank notes and deposits as what they are in economic and social fact: claims, warehouse receipts to standard money—in short, that the note and the deposit holders be recognized as owners-in-law of the gold (or, under a fiat standard, of the paper) in the bank's vaults. Now treated in law as a debt, a deposit or note should

---

[22]Professor Beckhart has recently called our attention to the long-standing and successful practice of Swiss banks of issuing debentures of varying maturities, and the recent adoption of this practice in Belgium and Holland. While Beckhart contemplates debentures for long-term loans only, I see no reason why banks cannot issue short-term debentures as well. If business needs short-term loans, it can finance them by competing with everyone else in the market for voluntarily saved funds. Why grant the short-term market the special privilege and subsidy of creating money? Benjamin H. Beckhart, "To Finance Term Loans," *New York Times*, May 31, 1960.

be considered as evidence of a bailment.[23] In relation to general legal principles this would not be a radical change, since warehouse receipts are treated as bailments now. Banks would simply be treated as money warehouses in relation to their notes and deposits.[24]

----

[23]"A *bailment* may be defined as the transfer of personal property to another person with the understanding that the property is to be returned when a certain purpose has been completed . . . In a sale, we relinquish both title and possession. In a bailment, we merely give up temporarily the possession of the goods." Robert O. Sklar and Benjamin W. Palmer, *Business Law* (New York: McGraw-Hill, 1942), p. 361.

Nussbaum surely begs the question when he says, "Only in a broad and non-technical sense may the relationship of the depositary bank to the depositor be considered a fiduciary one. No trust proper or bailment is involved. *The contrary view would lay an unbearable burden upon banking business*" (italics mine). But if such banking business is improper, this is precisely the sort of burden that should be imposed. This is but one example of what happens to jurisprudence when pragmatic considerations of "public policy" supplant the search for principles of justice. Arthur Nussbaum, *Money in the Law, National and International* (Brooklyn, N. Y.: Foundation Press, 1950), p. 105.

[24]On warehouse receipts as bailments, cf. William H. Spencer, *Casebook of Law and Business* (New York: McGraw-Hill, 1939), pp. 661ff.

Perhaps a proper legal system would also consider all "general deposit warrants" (which allow the warehouse to return any homogeneous good to the depositor) as really "specific deposit warrants," which, like bills of lading, establish ownership to specific, earmarked objects.

As Jevons, noting the superiority of specific deposit warrants and realizing their relationship to money, stated: "The most satisfactory kind of promissory document . . . is represented by bills of lading, pawn-tickets, dock-warrants, or certificates which establish ownership to a definite object . . . The important point concerning such promissory notes is, *that they cannot possibly be issued in excess of the goods actually deposited, unless by distinct fraud* [italics mine]. The issuer ought to act purely as a warehouse-keeper, and as

Professor Spahr often uses the analogy of a bridge to justify fractional-reserve money. The builder of a bridge estimates approximately how many people will be using it daily. He builds the bridge on that basis and does not attempt to accommodate all the people in the city, should they all decide to cross the bridge simultaneously. But the most critical fallacy of this analogy is that the inhabitants do not then have a legal claim to cross the bridge at any time. (This would be even more evident if the bridge were owned by a private firm.) On the other hand, the holders of money substitutes most emphatically do have a legal claim to their own property at any time they choose to redeem it. The claims must then be fraudulent, since the bank could not possibly meet them all.[25]

---

possession may be claimed at any time, he can never legally allow any object deposited to go out of his safe keeping until it is delivered back in exchange for the promissory note . . . More recently a better system [than general deposit warrant] has been introduced, and each specific lot of iron has been marked and set aside to meet some particular warrant. The difference seems to be slight, but it is really very important, as opening the way to a lax fulfillment of the contract . . . Moreover, it now [with general warrants] becomes possible to create a fictitious supply of a commodity, that is, to make people believe that a supply exists which does not exist . . . It used to be held as a general rule of law, that any present grant or assignment of goods not in existence is without operation" (*Money and the Mechanism of Exchange*, pp. 206–12; see also p. 221).

[25]A bank that fails is therefore not simply an entrepreneur whose forecasts have gone awry. It is a business whose betrayal of trust has finally been publicly revealed. Furthermore, a rule of every business is to adjust the time structure of its assets to the time structure of its liabilities, so that its assets on hand will match its liabilities due. The only exception to this rule is a bank, which lends at certain

To those who want the dollar convertible into gold but are content with the pre-1933 standard, we might cite the analysis of Amasa Walker, one of the great American economists a century ago: "So far as specie is held for the payment of these [fractional-reserve-backed] notes, this kind of currency is actually convertible, and equivalent to money; but, in so far as the credit element exceeds the specie, it is only a promise to pay money, and is inconvertible. A mixed [fractional-reserve] currency, therefore can only be regarded as partially convertible; the degree of its convertibility depending upon the proportion the specie bears to the notes issued and the deposits."[26]

For a believer in free enterprise, a system of "free banking" undoubtedly has many attractions. Not only does it seem most consistent with the general institution of free enterprise, but Mises and others have shown that free banking would lead not to the infinite supply of money envisioned by such Utopian partisans of free banking as Proudhoun, Spooner, Greene, and Meulen, but rather to a much "harder" and sounder money than exists when banks are controlled by a central bank. In

---

terms of maturities, while its liabilities are all instantly payable on demand. If a bank were to match the time structure of its assets and liabilities, all its assets would also have to be instantaneous, i.e., would have to be cash.

[26]*The Science of Wealth*, 3d ed. (Boston: Little, Brown, 1867), p. 139. In the same work, Walker presents a keen analysis of the defects and problems of a fractional-reserve currency (pp. 126–232).

practice, therefore, free banking would come much closer to the 100 percent ideal than the system we now have.[27] And yet if "free trade in banking is free trade in swindling," then surely the soundest course would be to take the swindling out of banking altogether. Mises's sole argument against 100 percent gold banking is that this would admit the unfortunate precedent of government control of the banking system. But if fractional-reserve banking is fraudulent, then it could be outlawed not as a form of administrative government intervention in the monetary system, but rather as part of the general legal prohibition of force and fraud.[28] Within this general prohibition of fraud, my proposed banking reform would leave the private banks entirely free.[29]

[27]See Mises, *Human Action*, pp. 439ff. Mises's position is that of the French economist Henri Cernuschi, who called for free banking as the best way of suppressing fiduciary bank credit: "I want to give everybody the right to issue banknotes so that nobody should take banknotes any longer" (ibid., p. 443). The German economist Otto Hübner held a similar position. See Smith, *Rationale of Central Banking*, passim.

[28]In short, our projected legal reform would fully comply with Mises's goal: "to place the banking business under the general rules of commercial and civil laws compelling every individual and firm to fulfill all obligations in full compliance with the terms of the contract" (*Human Action*, p. 440). Another point about free banking: to be tenable, it would have to be legal for 100 percent reserve partisans to establish "Anti-Bank Vigilante Leagues," publicly calling on all note and deposit holders to redeem their obligations because their banks were really and essentially bankrupt.

[29]Cf. Walker, pp. 230–31. In *A Program for Monetary Stability*, p. 108, Milton Friedman has expressed sympathy for the idea of free banking, but oddly enough only for deposits; notes he would leave as

Objections to 100 Percent Gold

Certain standard objections have been raised against 100 percent banking, and against 100 percent gold currency in particular. One generally accepted argument against any form of 100 percent banking I find particularly and strikingly curious: that under 100 percent reserves, banks would not be able to continue profitably in business. I see no reason why banks should not be able to charge their customers for their services, as do all other useful businesses. This argument points to the supposedly enormous benefits of banking; if these benefits were really so powerful, then surely the consumers would be willing to pay a service charge for them, just as they pay for traveler's checks now. If they were not willing to pay the costs of the banking business as they pay the costs of all other industries useful to them, then that would demonstrate the advantages of banking to have been highly overrated. At any rate, there is no reason why banking should not take its chance in the free market with every other industry.

The major objection against 100 percent gold is that this would allegedly leave the economy with an inadequate money supply. Some economists advocate a secular increase of the supply of money in accordance with some criterion: population growth, growth of volume of trade,

---

a government monopoly. It should be clear that there is no essential economic difference between notes and deposits. They differ in technological form only; economically, they are both promises to pay on demand in a fixed amount of standard money.

and the like; others wish the money supply to be adjusted to provide a stable and fixed price level. In both cases, of course, the adjusting and manipulating could only be done by government. These economists have not fully absorbed the great monetary lesson of classical economics: that the supply of money essentially does not matter. Money performs its function by being a medium of exchange; any change in its supply, therefore, will simply adjust itself in the purchasing power of the money unit, that is, in the amount of other goods that money will be able to buy. An increase in the supply of money means merely that more units of money are doing the social work of exchange and therefore that the purchasing power of each unit will decline. Because of this adjustment, money, in contrast to all other useful commodities employed in production or consumption, does not confer a social benefit when its supply increases. The only reason that increased gold mining is useful, in fact, is that the large supply of gold will satisfy more of the nonmonetary uses of the gold commodity.

There is therefore never any need for a larger supply of money (aside from the nonmonetary uses of gold or silver). An increased supply of money can only benefit one set of people at the expense of another set, and, as we have seen, that is precisely what happens when government or the banks inflate the money supply. And that is precisely what my proposed reform is designed to eliminate. There can, incidentally, never be an actual monetary "shortage," since the very fact that the market has established and continues to use gold or silver as a monetary commodity shows that enough of it exists to be useful as a medium of exchange.

The number of people, the volume of trade, and all other alleged criteria are therefore merely arbitrary and irrelevant with respect to the supply of money. And as for the ideal of the stable price level, apart from the grave flaws of deciding on a proper index, there are two points that are generally overlooked. In the first place, the very ideal of a stable price level is open to challenge. Hoarding, as we have indicated, is always attacked; and yet it is the freely expressed and desired action on the market. People often wish to increase the real value of their cash balances, or to raise the purchasing power of each dollar. There are many reasons why they might wish to do so. Why should they not have this right, as they have other rights on the free market? And yet only by their "hoarding" taking effect through lower prices can they bring about this result. Only by demanding more cash balances and thus lowering prices can the dollars assume a higher real value. I see no reason why government manipulators should be able to deprive the consuming public of this right. Second, if people really had an overwhelming desire for a stable price level, they would negotiate all their contracts in some agreed-upon price index. The fact that such a voluntary "tabular standard" has rarely been adopted is an apt enough commentary on those stable-price-level enthusiasts who would impose their ambitions by government coercion.

Money, it is often said, should function as a yardstick, and therefore its value should be stabilized and fixed. Not its value, however, but its *weight* should be eternally fixed, as are all other weights. Its value, like all other values, should be left to the judgment, estimation, and ultimate decision of every individual consumer.[30]

Professor Yeager and
100 Percent Gold

One of the most important discussions of the 100 percent gold standard in recent years is by Professor Leland Yeager.[31] Professor Yeager, while actually at the

---

[30]The totally neglected political theorist Isabel Paterson wrote as follows on the "compensated" or "commodity" dollar scheme of Irving Fisher, which would have juggled the weight of the dollar in order to stabilize its value: "As all units of measure are determined arbitrarily in the first place, though not fixed by law, obviously they can be altered by law. The same length of cotton could be designated an inch one day, a foot the next, and a yard the next; the same quantity of precious metal could be denominated ten cents today and a dollar tomorrow. But the net result would be that figures used on different days would not mean the same thing; and somebody must take a heavy loss. The alleged argument for a 'commodity dollar' was that a real dollar, of fixed quantity, will not always buy the same quantity of goods. Of course it will not. If there is no medium of value, no money, neither would a yard of cotton or a pound of cheese always exchange for an unvarying fixed quantity of any other goods. It was argued that a dollar ought always to buy the same quantity of and description of goods. It will not and cannot. That could occur only if the same number of dollars and the same quantities of goods of all kinds and in every kind were always in existence and in exchange and always in exactly proportionate demand; while if production and consumption were admitted, both must proceed constantly at an equal rate to offset one another" (*The God of the Machine* [New York: Putnam, 1943], p. 203n).

[31]Leland B. Yeager, "An Evaluation of Freely-Fluctuating Exchange Rates," unpublished Ph.D. dissertation, Columbia University, 1952.

opposite pole as an advocate of freely-fluctuating fiat moneys, recognizes the great superiority of 100 percent gold over the usual pre-1933 type of gold standard. The main objections to the gold standard are its vulnerability to great and sudden deflations and the difficulties that national authorities face when a specie drain abroad threatens domestic bank reserves and forces contraction. With 100 percent gold, Yeager recognizes, none of these problems would exist:

> Under a 100 percent hard-money international gold standard, the currency of each country would consist exclusively of gold (or of gold plus fully-backed warehouse receipts for gold in the form of paper money and token coins). The government and its agencies would not have to worry about any drain on their reserves. The gold warehouses would never be embarrassed by requests to redeem paper money in gold, since each dollar of paper money in circulation would represent a dollar of gold actually in a warehouse. There would be no such thing as independent national monetary policies; the volume of money in each country would be determined by market forces. The world's gold supply would be distributed among the various countries according to the demands for cash balances of the individuals in the various countries. There would be no danger of gold deserting some countries and piling up excessively in others, for each individual would take care not to let his cash balance shrink or expand to a size which he considered inappropriate in view of his own income and wealth.

> Under a 100 percent gold standard . . . the various countries would have a common monetary system, just as the various states of the United States now have a common monetary system. There would be no more reason to

worry about disequilibrium in the balance of payments of any particular country than there is now reason to worry about disequilibrium in the balance of payments of New York City. If each individual (and institution) took care to avoid persistent disequilibrium in his personal balance of payments, that would be enough . . . The actions of individuals in maintaining their cash balances at appropriate levels would "automatically" take care of the adequacy of each country's money supply.

The problems of national reserves, deflation, and so forth, Yeager points out, are due to the fractional-reserve nature of the gold standard, not to gold itself. "National fractional reserve systems are the real source of most of the difficulties blamed on the gold standard." With fractional reserves, individual actions no longer suffice to assure automatically the proper distribution of the supply of gold. "The difficulties arise because the mixed national currencies—currencies which are largely paper and only partly gold—are insufficiently international. The main defect of the historical gold standard is the necessity of 'protecting' national gold reserves." Central banking and its management only make things worse: "In short, whether a Central Bank amplifies the effects of gold flows, remains passive in the face of gold flows, or 'offsets' gold flows, its behavior is incompatible with the principles of the full-fledged gold standard . . . Indeed, any kind of monetary management runs counter to the principles of the pure gold standard."[32]

In view of this eloquent depiction of the 100 percent

---

[32]Ibid., pp. 9–17.

gold standard, why does Yeager flatly reject it and call instead for freely fluctuating fiat money? Largely because only with fiat money can each governmental unit stabilize the price level in its own area in times of depression. Now I cannot pause to discuss further the policy of stabilization, which I believe to be both fallacious and disastrous. I can only point out that contrary to Professor Yeager, price declines and exchange rate depreciation are not simple alternatives. To believe this is to succumb to a fatal methodological holism and to abandon the sound path of methodological individualism. If, for example, a steel union in a certain area is causing unemployment in steel by insisting on keeping its wage rates up though prices have fallen, I consider it at once unjust, a cause of misallocations and distortions of production, and positively futile to try to remedy the problem by forcing all the consumers in the area to suffer by paying higher prices for their imports (through a fall in the area's exchange rate).

One problem that every monetary statist and nationalist has failed to face is the geographical boundary of each money. If there should be national fluctuating fiat money, what should be the boundaries of the "nation"? Surely political frontiers have little or no economic meaning. Professor Yeager is courageous enough to recognize this and to push fiat money almost to a *reductio* by advocating, or at least considering, entirely separate moneys for each region or even locality in a nation.

Yeager has not pushed the *reductio* far enough, however. Logically, the ultimate in freely fluctuating fiat moneys is a different money issued by each and every individual. We have seen that this could not come about on the free market. But suppose that this came about by momentum from the present system or through some other method. What then? Then we would have a world chaos indeed, with "Rothbards," "Yeagers," "Joneses," and billions of other individual currencies freely fluctuating on the market. I think it would be instructive if some economist devoted himself to an intensive analysis of what such a world would look like. I think it safe to say that the world would be back to an enormously complex and chaotic form of barter and that trade would be reduced to a virtual standstill. For there would no longer be any sort of monetary medium for exchanges. Each separate exchange would require a different "money." In fact, since money *means* a general medium of exchanges, it is doubtful if the very concept of *money* would any longer apply. Certainly the indispensable economic calculation provided by the money and price system would have to cease, since there would no longer be a common unit of account.[33] This is a serious and not farfetched criticism of fiat-money proposals, because all of them introduce some of this chaotic

[33]Professor Yeager indeed concedes that an independent money for each person or firm would be going too far. "Beyond some admittedly indefinable point, the proliferation of separate currencies for ever smaller and more narrowly defined territories would begin to negate the very concept of money." But our contention is that the "indefinable point" is precisely definable as the very first point that fiat paper enters to break up the world's money. See Leland B. Yeager, "Exchange Rates within a Common Market," *Social Research* (Winter 1958): 436–37.

element into the world economy. In short, fluctuating fiat moneys are disintegrative of the very function of money itself. If every individual had his own money, the disintegration of the very existence of money would be complete; but national—and still more regional and local—fiat moneys already partially disintegrate the money medium. They contradict the essence of the monetary function.

Finally, Professor Yeager wonders why such "orthodox liberals" as Mises, Hayek, and Robbins should have insisted on the "monetary internationalism" of the gold standard. Without presuming to speak for them, I think the answer can be put in two parts: (1) because they favor monetary freedom rather than government management and manipulation of money, and (2) because they favored the existence of money as compared to barter—because they believed that money is one of the greatest and most significant features of the modern market economy, and indeed of civilization itself. The more general the money, the greater the scope for division of labor and for the interregional exchange of goods and services that stem from the market economy. A monetary medium is therefore critical to the free market, and the wider the use of this money, the more extensive the market and the better it can function. In short, true freedom of trade does require an international commodity money—as the history of the market economy of recent centuries has shown—gold and silver. Any breakup of such an international medium by statist fiat paper inevitably cripples and disintegrates the free market, and robs the world of the fruits of that market. Ultimately, the issue is a stark one: we can either return to gold or we can pursue the fiat path and return to barter. It is perhaps not hyperbole to say that civilization itself is at stake in our decision.[34]

The 100 Percent Gold Tradition

I therefore advocate as the soundest monetary system and the only one fully compatible with the free market and with the absence of force or fraud from any source a 100 percent gold standard. This is the only system compatible with the fullest preservation of the rights of property. It is the only system that assures the end of inflation and, with it, of the business cycle.[35] And it is the only form of gold standard that fully meets the following argument of the Douglas subcommittee

[34]Other criticisms by Yeager are really, as he recognizes at one point, criticisms of any plan for 100 percent banking, fiat or gold. There is, for example, the problem of how to suppress new forms of demand liabilities that might well arise to evade the legal restrictions. I do not think this an important argument. Fraud is always difficult to combat, and indeed continues in numerous forms to this day (as does all manner of crime). Does this mean that we should give up outlawing and punishing fraud and other crimes against person and property? Secondly, I am sure that the practical problems of law enforcement would be greatly reduced if the public were to receive a thorough education in the fundamentals of banking. If, in short, 100-percent-money advocates were allowed to form Anti-Bank Vigilante Leagues to point out the shakiness and immorality of fractional-reserve banking, the public would be much less inclined to evade such restrictions than it is now.

[35]*Pace* the Mises-Hayek theory of the trade cycle, which was shunted aside but not refuted by the Keynesian Revolution.

against a return to gold: "An overriding reason against making gold coin freely available is that no government [or banks?] should make promises . . . which it would not be able to keep if the demand should arise. Monetary systems for over a century . . . have expanded more rapidly than would be permitted by accretions of gold."[36]

While this is undoubtedly a "radical" program for this day and age, it is important to note briefly that this program is squarely in a great tradition: not only in the economic tradition of the classical economists and the currency school, but also in the American political tradition of the Jeffersonians and the Jacksonians. In essence, this was their program. In passing it should be noted that almost all historians, with the notable exceptions of William Graham Sumner and Joseph Dorfman, have misinterpreted the Jeffersonians and Jacksonians as economically ignorant and anti-capitalist agrarians lashing out at a credit system they failed to understand. Whether one agrees with their position or not, they wrote in full and sophisticated knowledge of classical economics and were fully devoted to capitalism and the free market, which they believed were hampered and not aided by the institution of fractional-reserve banking.[37] In fact, it

---

[36]*Report of the Subcommittee on Monetary, Credit, and Financial Policies of the Joint Committee on the Economic Report*, 81 Cong., 2 Sess. (Washington, 1950), pp. 41ff.

[37]The conservative economic historians of the late nineteenth century saw Jackson as an ignorant agrarian trying to destroy capitalism

might almost be said that these Americans were unterrified members of the currency school, lacking the almost blind devotion to the Bank of England of their more pragmatic British cousins. Indeed, the currency principle was enunciated in America several years before it made its appearance in England.[38] And such founders of the currency principle in America as Condy Raguet realized what the more eminent British tragically failed to see: that bank deposits are just as fully money substitutes as bank notes, and are therefore part of the broad money supply.[39]

---

and calling for inflation against the central bank. The progressives of the Beard school took much the same approach, except that they applauded the Jacksonians for their alleged anti-capitalist stand. The most recent Bray Hammond-Thomas Govan school have again shifted their praise to the Whigs and the Bank of the United States, which they view as essential to a modern credit system as against the absurdly hard-money views of the Jacksonians.

[38]During the Panic of 1819, for example—several years before Thomas Joplin's enunciation of the currency principle in England—Thomas Jefferson, John Adams, John Quincy Adams, Governor Thomas Randolph of Virginia, Daniel Raymond (author of the first treatise on economics in the United States), Condy Raguet, and Amos Kendall all wrote in favor of either a pure 100 percent gold money, or of 100 percent gold backing for paper. See Murray N. Rothbard, "The Panic of 1819: Contemporary Opinion and Policy," Ph.D. dissertation (Columbia University, 1956). John Adams considered the issue of paper beyond specie as "theft," and Raymond called the practice a "stupendous fraud." Similar views were held by the important French ideologue and economist, and friend of Jefferson, Count Destutt de Tracy. Cf. Michael J. L. O'Connor, *Origins of Academic Economics in the United States* (New York: Columbia University Press, 1944), pp. 28, 38.

[39]Failure of the British currency school to realize this led to the discrediting of Peel's Act of 1844, which required 100 percent reserve for all further issue of bank notes, but left bank deposits completely free.

After the Civil War, hard-money economists were preoccupied with battling the new greenback and free-silver problems, and the idea of 100 percent gold virtually faded from view. General Amasa Walker, however, wrote into the 1860s and even he was surpassed in acumen by the brilliant and neglected writings of the Boston merchant Charles H. Carroll, who advocated 100 percent gold reserves against bank deposits as well as notes, and also urged the replacement of the name "dollar" by gold ounce or gold gram.[40] And an official of the United States Assay Office, Isaiah W. Sylvester, who has been completely neglected by historians, advocated a 100 percent dollar and parallel standards.[41] In the present century the only economist to advocate a 100 percent gold standard, to my knowledge, has been Dr. Elgin Groseclose.[42]

[40]On Carroll, see Lloyd W. Mints, *A History of Banking Theory* (Chicago: University of Chicago Press, 1945), pp. 129, 135ff., 155–56; and especially the collection of Carroll's writings, *Organization of Debt into Currency and Other Papers*, Edward C. Simmons, ed. (Salem, N.Y.: Ayer, 1972).

[41]Isaiah W. Sylvester, *Bullion Certificates as Currency* (New York, 1882). On parallel standards, also see Brough, *Open Mints and Free Banking*, passim. For Brough's attack on the disruption caused by independent currency names, see ibid., p. 93.

[42]Thus Groseclose: "The practice of the goldsmiths, of using deposited funds to their own interest and profit, was essentially unsound, if not actually dishonest and fraudulent. A warehouseman, taking goods deposited with him and devoting them to his own profit, either by use or by loan to another, is guilty of a tort, a conversion of goods for which he is liable in . . . law. By a casuistry which is now elevated into an economic principle, but which has no defenders outside the

Murray N. Rothbard

The Road Ahead

Having decided to return to a 100 percent gold dollar, we are confronted with the problem of how to go about it. There is no question about the difficulty of the transition period required to reach our goal. But once the transition period is concluded, we will have the

---

realm of banking, a warehouseman who deals in money is subject to a diviner law: the banker is free to use for his private interest and profit the money left in trust . . .

"Sooner or later we must abandon the pretense that we can eat our cake and have it, that we may have money on deposit ready to be withdrawn at any moment, and at the same time loaned out in a thousand diverse enterprises, and recognize that the only assurance of liquidity of bank deposits is to have the actual money waiting on the depositor at whatever moment he may appear. This would not mean the extinction of credit, nor the disappearance of lending institutions. But it would mean the divorcement of credit from the money mechanism, the cessation . . . of the use of credit instruments as media of exchange . . . It would mean the disappearance of the most insidious form of fictitious credit. We could still have investment banking, providing credit at long term, and bill brokers and finance companies, providing credit at short term; but such credit would not be the transfer of a fictitious purchasing power drawn from the reservoirs of a banking system whose own sources derive from the use of the bank check; the credit available would be true credit, that is, the transfer of actual, existing wealth in exchange for wealth to be created and returned at a future time. Such credit would not be inflationary, as is bank credit, for every dollar made available as purchasing power to the borrower would be the result of the abstinence from the exercise of purchasing power on the part of the lender; it would be merely the transfer of purchasing power, not the creation of purchasing power by fiction" (*Money, The Human Conflict* [Norman: University of Oklahoma Press, 1934], pp. 178, 273).

Professor F. A. Hayek, in his *Monetary Nationalism and International Stability* (New York: Longmans, Green, 1937), was highly

satisfaction of possessing the best monetary system known to man and of eliminating inflation, business cycles, and the uneconomic and immoral practice of people acquiring money at the expense of producers. Since we have many times the number of dollars as we have gold dollars at the present fixed weight of the dollar, we have essentially two alternative, polar routes toward 100 percent gold: either to force a deflation of the supply of dollars down to the currently valued gold stock, or to "raise the price of gold" (to lower the definition of the dollar's weight) to make the total stock of gold dollars 100 percent equal to the total supply of dollars in the society. Or we can choose some combination of the two routes.

---

sympathetic to 100 percent gold, and demonstrated, in some excellent analysis, the superiority of 100 percent gold to the mixed, fractional-reserve gold standard, and to independent fiat moneys. In the end, he apparently set aside the proposal because of the difficulties of bank evasion; moreover, he concluded, rather inconsistently, by considering the ideal monetary system as directed by an international central bank, with the gold standard as only second best. Robbins, while discussing 100 percent money, was more sympathetic to free banking under a gold standard. Lionel Robbins, *Economic Planning and International Order* (London: Macmillan, 1937), pp. 269–305. In recent years, Hayek has abandoned the gold standard completely on behalf of a composite-commodity standard: "A Commodity Reserve Currency," in his *Individualism and Economic Order* (Chicago: University of Chicago Press, 1948), pp. 209–19. Since Hayek's major reason for the shift is that the total supply of gold is not flexible enough to change when demanded (and since, even in his earlier work, Hayek wrote of a "rationally" determined total supply of world money, regulated by an international monetary authority), it is clear that Hayek does not see that no specific total supply of money is better than any other, and that therefore no government manipulation of the supply is desirable.

Professor Spahr and his associates wish to return to the gold standard (though not to 100 percent gold) at the current "price" of $35 an ounce, stressing the importance of fixity of the weight of the dollar. If these were before 1933 and we were still on a gold standard, even if a defective one, I would unhesitatingly agree. The principle of a fixed weight for the dollar, and above all the principle of the sanctity of contract, are essential to our entire system of private property, and therefore would have been well worth the difficulties of a severe deflation. Aside from that, we have built deflation into an absurd ogre, and have overlooked the healthy consequences of a deflationary purgation of the malinvestments of the boom, as well as the overdue aid that fixed income groups, hit by decades of inflationary erosion, would at last obtain from a considerable fall in prices. A sharp deflation would also help to break up the powerful aggregations of monopoly unionism, which are potentially so destructive of the market economy. At any rate, while the deflation would be nominally sharp, to the extent that people would wish to save much of their present cash holdings, they would increase voluntary savings by purchasing bank debentures in lieu of their deposits, thereby fostering "economic growth" and mitigating the rigors of the deflation.

On the other hand, there is no particular reason to be devoted to the $35 figure at the present time, since the existing "gold standard" and definition of the dollar are only applicable to foreign governments and central banks; as far as the people are concerned, we are now on a virtual fiat standard. Therefore, we may change the definition of the dollar as a preliminary step to return to a full gold standard, and we would not really be disturbing the principle of fixity. As in the case of any definition of weight, the *initial* definition is purely arbitrary, and we are so close now to a fiat standard that we may consider any dollar in a new standard as an initial definition.

Depending on how we define the money supply—and I would define it very broadly as all claims to dollars at fixed par value—a rise in the gold price sufficient to bring the gold stock to 100 percent of total dollars would require a ten- to twentyfold increase. This of course would bring an enormous windfall gain to the gold miners, but this does not concern us. I do not believe that we should refuse an offer of a mass entry into Heaven simply because the manufacturers of harps and angels' wings would enjoy a windfall gain. But certainly a matter for genuine concern would be the enormous impetus such a change would give for several years to the mining of gold, as well as the disruption it would cause in the pattern of international trade.

Which course we take, or which particular blend of the two, is a matter for detailed study by economists. Obviously little or none of this needed study has been undertaken. I therefore do not propose here a detailed blueprint. I would like to see all of those who have become convinced of the need for a 100 percent gold standard join in such a study of the best path to take toward such a goal under present conditions. Broadly, the desired program may be summarized as follows:

1. Arrival of a 100 percent gold dollar, either by deflation of dollars to a gold stock valued at $35 per ounce, or by revaluation of the dollar at a "gold price" high enough to make the gold stock 100 percent of the present supply of dollars, or a blend of the two routes.

2. Getting the gold stock out of the hands of the government and into the hands of the banks and the people, with the concomitant liquidation of the Federal Reserve System, and a legal 100 percent requirement for all demand claims.

3. The transfer of all note-issue functions from the Treasury and the Federal Reserve to the private banks. All banks, in short, would be allowed to issue deposits *or* notes at the discretion of their clients.

4. Freeing silver bullion and its representative in silver certificates (which would now be issued by the banks) from any fixed value in gold. In short, silver ounces and their warehouse receipts would fluctuate, as do all other commodities, on the market in terms of gold or dollars, thus giving us "parallel" gold and silver moneys, with gold dollars presumably remaining the chief money as the unit of account.

5. The eventual elimination of the term "dollar," using only terms of weight such as "gold gram" or "gold ounce."[43]

[43]For an eloquent for plea for using pure units of weight for money instead of national names, see Jean-Baptiste Say, *A Treatise on Political Economy*, New American ed. (Philadelphia: Grigg and

The ultimate goal would be the return to gold by every nation, at 100 percent of its particular currency, and the subsequent blending of all these national currencies into one unified world gold-gram unit. This was one of the considered goals at the abortive international monetary conferences of the late nineteenth century.[44] In such a world, there would be no exchange rates except between gold and silver, for the national currency names would be abandoned for simple weights of gold, and all the world's money would at long last be freed from government intervention.

6. Free (but presumably not gratuitous) private coinage of gold and silver.

I must here differ with Professor Mises's and Henry Hazlitt's suggestion for return to the gold standard by first establishing a "free market" in gold by cutting the dollar completely loose from gold, and then seeing, after several years, what gold price the market would

---

Elliot, 1841), pp. 256ff. Say also favored a freely fluctuating market between gold and silver.

More recently, Everett R. Taylor has advocated private coinage of gold and silver, and a 100 percent gold dollar, while another writer, Oscar B. Johannsen, has favored private coinage and free banking under a gold standard. Taylor, *Progress Report on a New Bill of Rights* (Diablo, Calif.: privately published, 1954); Johannsen, "Advocates Unrestricted Private Control Over Money and Banking," *Commercial and Financial Chronicle* (June 12, 1958): 2622ff.

[44]See Barnard, *Metric System of Weights and Measures*, and Henry B. Russell, *International Monetary Conferences* (New York: Harper, 1898), p. 61.

establish.[45] In the first place, this would cut the last tenuous link that the dollar still has to gold and yield us a totally fiat money. Second, the market would hardly be a "free" one, since almost all the nation's gold would be sequestered in government hands. I think it important to move in the reverse direction. The Federal government, after all, seized the people's gold in 1933 under the guise of a temporary emergency. It is important, for moral and economic reasons, to permit the people to reclaim their gold as rapidly as possible. And since the gold is still held as hostage for our dollars, I believe that the official link and official convertibility between dollars and gold should be re-established as soon as Congress can be so persuaded. And finally, since the dollar is merely a weight of gold, properly speaking, it is not at all appropriate to establish a "market" between dollars and gold, any more than there should be a "market" between one-dollar bills and five-dollar bills.

There is no gainsaying the fact that this suggested program will strike most people as impossibly "radical" and "unrealistic"; any suggestion for changing the status quo, no matter how slight, can always be considered by someone as too radical, so that the only thoroughgoing escape from the charge of impracticality is never to advocate any change whatever in existing conditions. But to take this approach is to abandon human reason, and to drift in animal- or plant-like manner with the tide

---

[45]Mises, *The Theory of Money and Credit*, pt. 4; and Henry Hazlitt, *Return to Gold* (New York: *Newsweek*, 1954).

of events. As Professor Philbrook pointed out in a brilliant article some years ago, we must frame our policy convictions on what we believe the best course to be and then try to convince others of this goal, and not include within our policy conclusions estimates of what other people may find acceptable.[46] For *someone* must propagate the truth in society, as opposed to what is politically expedient. If scholars and intellectuals fail to do so, if they fail to expound their convictions of what they believe the correct course to be, they are abandoning truth, and therefore abandoning their very *raison d'être*. All hope of social progress would then be gone, for no new ideas would ever be advanced nor effort expended to convince others of their validity.

---

[46]Clarence Philbrook, "'Realism' in Policy Espousal," *American Economic Review* (December 1953): 846–59.

Index